VW BUS
ROAD
TO FREEDOM

IMPRESSUM

Copyright © 2008
by edel entertainment GmbH · Hamburg / Germany
Please see index for individual photographic
copyright. Please see tracklist credits for music
copyrights.

All rights whatsoever in this work and the
photographs are strictly reserved. No part of this
book may be reproduced in any form without the
prior consent of the publishers.

ISBN 978-3-940004-55-0

EDITORIAL DIRECTION
Jos Bendinelli Negrone / edel

CONCEPT, PHOTO EDITORIAL
AND MUSIC SELECTION:
Jos Bendinelli Negrone / edel

ART DIRECTION AND GRAPHIC DESIGN
Wolfgang Seidl · SEIDLDESIGN

TRANSLATION
ar.pege translations sprl

PRODUCED BY
optimal media production GmbH, Röbel / Germany
Printed and manufactured in Germany

earBOOKS is a division of
edel entertainment GmbH
For more information about earBOOKS please visit
www.earbooks.net

"ONE PILL MAKES YOU LARGER AND ONE PILL MAKES YOU SMALL AND THE ONES THAT MOTHER GIVES YOU DON'T DO ANYTHING AT ALL GO ASK ALICE WHEN SHE'S TEN FEET TALL"

JEFFERSON AIRPLANE · *White Rabbit* · (CD 2 | TRACK 1)

"PURPLE HAZE ALL IN MY BRAIN, LATELY THINGS DON´T SEEM THE SAME. ACTIN´ FUNNY BUT I DON´T KNOW WHY. ´SCUSE ME WHILE I KISS THE SKY"

JIMI HENDRIX · *Purple Haze* (CD 1 | TRACK 16)

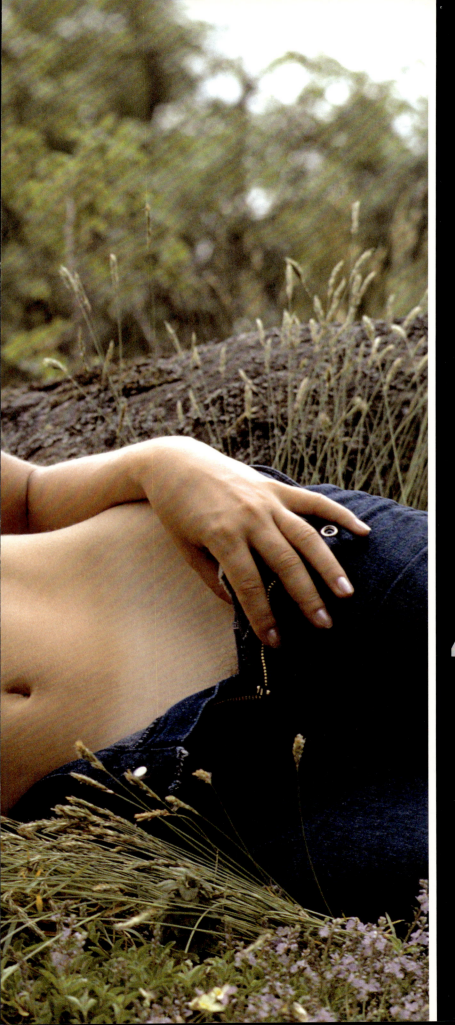

" IF YOU´RE GOING TO
SAN FRANCISCO,
BE SURE TO WEAR A
FLOWER
IN YOUR HAIR "

SCOTT McKENZIE · *San Francisco*

"**ALL YOU LADIES** ARE ON YOUR WAY TO CHURCH (I'M BEGGIN') WILL I JUST BE A' ROAMIN LOOKIN FOR THE THING THAT I **SEARCH**"

NEW YORK DOLLS · *Looking For A Kiss* (CD 1 | TRACK 8)

23

" **ME AND YOU** AND A DOG NAMED **BOO,** TRAVELLIN' AND LIVIN' OFF THE LAND. ME AND YOU AND A DOG NAMED BOO, HOW I LOVE BEIN' A FREE MAN. "

LOBO · *Me and You And A Dog Named Boo* (CD 1 | TRACK 6)

27

"LOVE IS ALL YOU NEED"

THE BEATLES · *All You Need Is Love*

"ALL WE ARE SAYING IS GIVE PEACE A CHANCE"

JOHN LENNON

"YOU´RE EITHER ON THE BUS OR OFF THE BUS"

KEN KESEY

" FOR TEN WEEKS NOW NUMBER THREE STOOD EMPTY
NOBODY THOUGHT THERE WOULD BE
FAMILY LAUGHTER BEHIND THE WINDOWS
OR A CHRISTMAS TREE.
THEN A COUPLE FROM UP NORTH
SORROW AND HIS WIFE ARRIVED
BEFORE THE SUN HAD LEFT THE STREETS
THEY WERE LIVING INSIDE. "

PRETTY THINGS · *SF Sorrow Is Born* (CD 2 | TRACK 2)

"WHENEVER **YOU** **FIND** YOURSELF ON THE **SIDE** OF THE MAJORITY, IT´S TIME TO PAUSE **AND** REFLECT"

MARK TWAIN

WE DO HATE
RACE-MIXING
LINCOLN ROCKWELL'S
'HATE' BUS
372·648
1961 VIRGINIA
MILITARY POL
156P

"**THEY** WON'T GIVE **PEACE** A CHANCE, **THAT'S** JUST A **DREAM** SOME OF US HAD"

JONI MITCHELL

LOVE
BUS

" NOW THE ONLY THING A GAMBLER NEEDS IS A SUITCASE AND A TRUNK AND THE ONLY TIME HE'S SATISFIED IS WHEN HE'S ON A DRUNK "

ERIC BURDON · *House Of The Rising Sun* (CD 1 | TRACK 3)

Zwei Wagen in einem –

VW-Kombi

"IF LOVIN' YOU IS WRONG, I DON'T WANT TO BE RIGHT.."

PERCY SLEDGE · *If Loving You Is Wrong* (CD 1 | TRACK 12)

"GIVE ME A TICKET FOR AN AEROPLANE
AIN'T GOT TIME TO TAKE A FAST TRAIN
LONELY DAYS ARE GONE, I'M A-GOIN' HOME
MY BABY JUST WROTE ME A LETTER"

THE BOX TOPS · *The Letter* (CD 1 | TRACK 2)

" ZERO… WHERE ARE YOU?…
DON'T YOU REMEMBER WHY YOU CAME TO
EVERYWHERE?…
THE PIECE OF MIND THAT YOU CAME TO FIND HAS
DISAPPEARED…"

GONG · *You Never Blow Your Trip Forever* (CD 2 | TRACK 6)

"THE MOST IMPORTANT KIND OF FREEDOM IS TO BE WHAT YOU REALLY ARE"

JIM MORRISON

VW-Transporter helfen Geld verdienen

"I WALK ALONE IN DREAMS,
I CANNOT FEEL,
I CANNOT SEE'
THE ONLY THING I KNOW IS THAT
YOU'RE
ONLY REAL TO ME"

THE TROGGS · *Night Of The Long Grass* (CD 1 | TRACK 1)

"SUN IS SHINING, THE WEATHER IS SWEET, MAKE YOU WANNA MOVE YOUR DANCING FEET NOW TO THE RESCUE, HERE I AM WANT YOU TO KNOW, Y'ALL, CAN YOU UNDERSTAND?"

BOB MARLEY & THE WAILERS · *Sun Is Shining* (CD I | TRACK II)

"**YOU** CREATE **YOUR OWN** REALITY"

SETH SPEAKS

"RIDE, RIDE, RIDE, HITCHIN' A RIDE"

Mit der ganzen

VW.-Kleinbus...

Familie unterwegs - sorglos und unabhängig

der große Volkswagen für kleine Gesellschaften

" I TOOK THE ROAD
LESS
TRAVELLED BY,
AND THAT HAS'
MADE
ALL THE
DIFFERENCE"

ROBERT FROST

"IF YOU CAN REMEMBER THE 60^S, THEN YOU WEREN´T THERE"

UNKNOWN

"I'M SO TIRED OF **CRYING,** BUT I'M OUT ON THE ROAD **AGAIN**"

CANNED HEAT · *On The Road Again*
(CD I | TRACK 13)

"**ME AND YOU AND YOU AND ME NO MATTER HOW THEY TOSS THE DICE, IT HAD TO BE THE ONLY ONE FOR ME IS YOU, AND YOU FOR ME SO HAPPY TOGETHER**"

THE TURTLES · *Happy Together*
(CD I | TRACK 5)

93

"YOU KNOW THE FIRST TIME I TRAVELED OUT IN THE RAIN AND SNOW, I DIDN'T HAVE NO PAYROLL, NOT EVEN NO PLACE TO GO."

CANNED HEAT · *On The Road Again* (CD I | TRACK 13)

"GO
CONFIDENTLY
IN THE
DIRECTION
OF YOUR
DREAMS.
LIVE
THE LIFE
YOU´VE
ALWAYS
IMAGINED"

HENRY DAVID THOREAU

VW BUS · ROAD TO FREEDOM
TRACK LISTING

CD1 ON THE ROAD

1. 03:04 — THE TROGGS · *Night Of The Long Grass (Reg Presley)*
Published by Polygram International Publishing Inc. (ASCAP)
Courtesy of Dominion Entertainment Inc. | (P) Dominion Entertainment Inc.

2. 01:55 — THE BOX TOPS · *The Letter (Wayne Carson Thompson)*
Published by Budde Songs Inc. (BMI)
Courtesy of Dominion Entertainment Inc. | (P) Dominion Entertainment Inc.

3. 02:52 — ERIC BURDON · *House Of The Rising Sun (Trad.)*
Published by Far Out Music Inc. | Muphise Music | (P) One Media Publishing

4. 03:08 — EDISON LIGHTHOUSE · *Spirit In The Sky (Norman Greenbaum)*
Published by Great Honesty Music Inc. | (P) One Media Publishing

5. 02:54 — THE TURTLES · *Happy Together (Bonner · Gordon)*
Published by EMI Publishing
Courtesy of Dominion Entertainment Inc. | (P) Dominion Entertainment Inc.

6. 03:06 — LOBO · *Me And You And A Dog Named Boo (R. La Voie)*
Published by Famous Music Publishing Co. (ASCAP)
Courtesy of Dominion Entertainment Inc. | (P) Dominion Entertainment Inc.

7. 02:39 — THE DRIFTERS · *Under The Boardwalk (Art Resnick · Kenny Young)*
Published by TM-MUSIC INC./TM MUSIC LTD. | (P) One Media Publishing

8. 03:28 — NEW YORK DOLLS · *Looking For A Kiss (David Johansen)*
Published by Lipstick Killers Publ Inc./ WB Music Corp/ Seldak Music Corp | (P) One Media Publishing

9. 02:52 — VANITY FARE · *Hitching A Ride (Callander · Murray)*
Published by Universal – Polygram International Publishing Inc. (BMI)
Courtesy of Dominion Entertainment Inc. | (P) Dominion Entertainment Inc.

10. 03:04 — AARON NEVILLE · *Waiting For A Bus (Warren Lee Taylor)*
Published by Screen Gems-EMI Music Inc. | (P) One Media Publishing

11. 02:12 — BOB MARLEY & THE WAILERS · *Sun Is Shining (Lee Perry · Bob Marley)*
An original Lee Perry recording
Published by Odnil MusicLtd./Fifty Six Hope Road Music | (P) Licensemusic.co ApS

12. 03:41 — PERCY SLEDGE · *If Loving You Is Wrong (Banks · Jackson · Hampton)*
Published by Irving Berlin Music Corp. (ASCAP)
Courtesy of Dominion Entertainment Inc. | (P) Dominion Entertainment Inc.

LIVE BONUS TRACKS

13. 05:07 — CANNED HEAT · *On The Road Again (Alan Wilson · Floyd Jones)*
Published by Frederick Music Company | (P) One Media Publishing

14. 04:50 — COMMANDER CODY AND THE LOST PLANET AIRMAN
Truck Driving Man (Terry Fell)
Published by American Music Inc./ Cross Music Ltd. | (P) One Media Publishing

15. 05:27 — ERIC BURDON · *Tobacco Road (John Loudermilk)*
Published by Cedarwood Publishing | (P) One Media Publishing

16. 03:03 — THE JIMI HENDRIX EXPERIENCE · *Purple Haze (Jim Hendrix)*
Published by Experience Hendrix LLC
An original Everest Records Group/Last Experience Inc. recording | (P) Licensemusic.co ApS

CD2 BREAK

1. 02:32 — JEFFERSON AIRPLANE · *White Rabbit (Slick)*
Published by Irving Music Inc. / Copperpenny Music
Courtesy of Excel Music Inc. | (P) Licensemusic.co ApS

2. 03:12 — THE PRETTY THINGS · *SF Sorrow Is Born (May · Taylor - Waller)*
Published by Lupus Music Company Ltd | (P) Snapper Music

3. 05:07 — THE 13TH FLOOR ELEVATORS · *Roller Coaster (Hall - Erickson)*
Published by Tapier Music Corp./BMI Houston, Texas/Dying Art Ltd/Int. Artists
An original International Artist recording | (P) Licensemusic.co ApS

4. 03:18 — BRIGITTE FONTAINE · *Apres La Guerre (Unknown)*
Published by Copyright Control
An original BYG recording | (P) Licensemusic.co ApS

5. 10:20 — GONG · *The Isle Of Everywhere*
(Howlett · Moerlen · Allen · Blake · Malherbe · Hillage · Smyth)
Published by Virgin Music Pub. Ltd./Byg
Extracted from the CD You
An original BYG recordingn | (P) Licensemusic.co ApS

6. 11:14 — GONG · *You Never Blow Your Trip Forever*
(Howlett · Moerlen · Allen · Blake · Malherbe · Hillage · Smyth)
Published by Virgin Music Pub. Ltd./Byg
Extracted from the CD You
An original BYG recordingn | (P) Licensemusic.co ApS

7. 08:20 — OZRIC TENTACLES · *Eternal Wheel (Wynne / Pepler)*
Published by Ed Wynne / Merv Pepler | (P) Snapper Music

VW T-MODELS

T1

1950 - 1967

The success story of the first VW Bus to go into series production started on the 8th of March 1950, subsequent to a drawing by Ben Pon. A completely new category of vehicle was created with the Bulli, one which is still enjoying great popularity today. The characteristic features of the T1 were the tapered V-shaped front with the large VW logo as well as the two-part front windshield. Around 1.82 million T1 models in various versions were produced up to 1976.

T2

1967 - 1979

The success story continued unwaveringly with model T2 of the VW Transporter. This second generation of Bullis demonstrated that a transporter was not just a vehicle, it was more the reflection of an attitude towards life. In Germany alone around 2.93 million units were built until 1979. The T2 thus has the highest production numbers for a VW Bus. Production also ran extremely well at the works in Brazil, South Africa and Mexico. External changes on the T2 were the revamped front with an integrated ventilation grill and a one-piece convex windscreen.

T3

1979 - 1990

The angular T3 with its characteristic box shape first came onto the market as petrol and also as diesel versions. Further technological innovations were the previously unknown four-wheel drive as well as replacement of the air-cooled boxer motors with water-cooled engines. The T3 set new yardsticks in family and leisure sectors, being primarily used as a "family van" or a camper. Until 1990 around two million models of the T3 were produced. In South Africa, production of the there very popular T3 even continued until 2003.

T4

1990 - 2003

The fourth generation of VW Buses brought to an end the era of rear-wheel drive and rear engines at Volkswagen. With this, the front motor, together with front-wheel drive, stood at the head of the technical innovations. For the first time the VW Bus was also available in three versions, with different chassis lengths and wheelbases. The transporter was predominantly used by firms and authorities, but at the same time it continued to be used as a touring vehicle, as its practical interior offered much convenience on tours.

T5

since 2003

As with its predecessors, the VW T5 has enjoyed great popularity since 2003. This model is also fitted with a transverse front motor and front-wheel drive. In addition to conversions of the T5 to emergency vehicles, for example, for the federal police as well as emergency doctor vehicles for the fire departments, in the last few years elegant special models have repeatedly appeared, such as the Caravelle, Multivan and the California.

VW T-MODELLE

T1

1950 - 1967

Die Erfolgsgeschichte und der damit als erster in Serie gehende VW Bus begann am 8. März 1950 nach einer Zeichnung von Ben Pon. Mit dem Bulli entstand eine völlig neue Fahrzeuggattung, die bis heute große Erfolge feiert. Die charakteristischen Merkmale des T1 waren das V-förmig zugelaufene Bug mit dem großen VW-Logo sowie die zweigeteilte Frontscheibe. Bis 1967 wurden rund 1,82 Millionen Modelle des T1 in diversen Ausführungen gefertigt.

T2

1967 - 1979

Mit dem Modell T2 des VW Transporters setzte sich der Erfolg beständig fort. Die zweite Generation des Bullis zeigte, dass der Transporter nicht bloß ein Fahrzeug ist, sondern vielmehr ein Lebensgefühl widerspiegelte. Allein in Deutschland wurden bis 1979 rund 2,93 Millionen Einheiten hergestellt. Somit ist der T2 der meistgebaute VW Bus aller Zeiten. Auch in den Werken Brasilien, Südafrika und Mexico verlief die Produktion äußerst erfolgreich. Äußere Veränderungen des T2 waren die neu konstruierte Frontpartie mit integriertem Lüftergrill und einer durchgehend gewölbten Frontscheibe.

T3

1979 - 1990

Der eckige T3 mit seiner typischen Kastenform kam erstmals als Benziner sowie auch als Dieselversion auf den Markt. Weitere technische Erneuerungen waren der vorher noch nicht dagewesene Allradantrieb sowie die Ersetzung von Luftboxer-Motoren durch wassergekühlte Aggregate. Im Familien- und Freizeitbereich setzte der T3 neue Maßstäbe und wurde vorwiegend als „Familienvan" oder Campingfahrzeug genutzt. Bis 1990 wurden rund zwei Millionen Modelle des T3 gefertigt. In Südafrika dauerte die Produktion des dort so beliebten T3 sogar bis 2003 an.

T4

1990 - 2003

Mit der vierten Generation des VW Busses ging bei Volkswagen die Ära des Heckantriebs und des Heckmotors zu Ende. Somit stand der Frontmotor mitsamt dem Frontantrieb im Vordergrund der technischen Erneuerungen. Erstmals war der VW Bus auch in drei unterschiedlich langen Karosserieversionen und Radständen erhältlich. Der Transporter wurde in erster Linie von Firmen und Behörden genutzt, gleichzeitig aber auch weiterhin als Reisemobil, da seine praktische Innenausstattung viel Komfort für Reisen bot.

T5

seit 2003

Wie auch schon seine Vorgänger erfreut sich der VW T5 seit 2003 großer Beliebtheit. Auch dieses Modell verfügt nach wie vor über einen quer eingebauten Frontmotor und einen Vorderradantrieb. Neben der Umrüstung des T5 zu Einsatzfahrzeugen wie beispielsweise der Bundespolizei sowie Notarzteinsatzfahrzeugen der Feuerwehr, erschienen in den letzten Jahren auch immer wieder elegante Sondermodelle wie der Caravelle, Multivan und der California.

PHOTOCREDITS

VW NUTZFAHRZEUGE PRESSE
PAGE: 4 · 6 · 7 · 10 · 22 · 29 · 34 · 36 · 42 · 48 · 54 · 58 · 60 · 65
68 · 70 · 72 · 75 · 76 · 80 · 83 · 85 · 92 · 98 · 101 · 103

D. KREUTZKAMP
PAGE: 25 · 41 · 45 · 50

CORBIS
PAGE: 3 · 12 · 14 · 16 · 19 · 21 · 30 · 46 · 52 · 56 · 66 · 89 · 91 · 97

PICTURE PRESS
PAGE: 9 · 32

PICTURE ALLIANCE
PAGE: 26 · 78 · 94

ULLSTEIN BILD
PAGE: 38 · 87

MAURITIUS IMAGES
PAGE: 62

SPECIAL THANKS TO:
VOLKSWAGEN NUTZFAHRZEUGE

" … WE CONDEMNED THEM, 'OUR CHILDREN,' FOR SEEKING A' DIFFERENT FUTURE. WE HATED THEM FOR THEIR FLOWERS, FOR THEIR LOVE,' AND FOR THEIR UNMISTAKEABLE' REJECTION OF EVERY HIDEOUS, MISTAKEN COMPROMISE' THAT WE HAD MADE THROUGHOUT OUR HOLLOW, MONEY-BITTEN, FRIGHTENED, ADULT LIVES "

JUNE JORDAN